Moments to Remember

'Priceless, and too precious to forget.'

Lucille Maye

Trafford rev. 05/08/2017

North America & international
toll-free: 1 888 232 4444 (USA & Canada)
fax: 812 355 4082

Dedication

This book is dedicated to my daughter, Sandy, and my grandson, Brandon. You both are the apple of my eye and I am so blessed and very fortunate to be part of your lives. To be your mom and grandmother is the most precious thing on earth to me. Thank you so much for your never-ending patience and understanding as I made preparations to write this book. Thank you so much more for believing in me and the encouragement you gave which caused me to believe in myself, that if I really wanted to I could do it. So, this is to you both with all my love.

Love, Mom (Gram)

Acknowledgements

Brandon Thompson – your gift of understanding and ability to comprehend my thoughts are most precious to me. Your capability to pick up my thoughts and to put them in legible form is amazing. Also, many thanks for your time, patience and the talent you have put forth to make this book a reality. A million thanks for your effort, without which, I might still be at the starting gate.

Introduction

Have you ever been a part of a large crowd of people or been in a position where you could watch people as they hurried to and fro? Have you wondered who they are, where they are going, what thoughts fill their minds as they hurried along? What specific moment or moments stand out in their memory as very special and precious to them? Who are important to them and to whom are they important? If one day they were gone, who among us might know what they really felt inside, what may have lain hidden deep within their soul?

The purpose of this book is to stir up your memory and to cause you to record some of the most important moments that have a significant and precious meaning to you that you have not had the chance to express. Life passes so swiftly and so many things need to be shared, but our daily routines and schedules do not always allow for such times of personal expression. And, so many times emotional moments of love, joy, hope and matters of the heart go unsaid and unnoticed, only to be covered over or buried somewhere in the recesses of the mind and heart for another time, if ever to emerge at all.

Even if such moments can never be shared while we are here, or maybe just briefly mentioned at occasional gatherings, wouldn't it be wonderful to leave such a special personal part of us behind that family and friends need only to read a few pages to catch a glimpse of who we really were, to understand much more the person who in some way shared their own lives? I would like to think so.

So, to get us started, I have recorded a very few of the moments that for me are priceless and too precious to forget. It is my hope that you will like this idea and fill the remaining pages with your personal Moments to Remember.

Life, Time and Purpose

Life is the most beautiful gift we will ever receive. Time is the scale by which life is measured. Purpose is the reason for which life is given. In the windows of time, there must always be MOMENTS TO REMEMBER, otherwise each nanosecond ticks away the seconds, minutes and hours that measure the weeks, months, years and centuries very methodically until all the allotted time for the specific purpose of life is used up. Time passes, and without a significant record or recollection of the events of life, we surely have only existed.

Sure, there are great historical moments when decisions are made by the governments of the world which change the courses and futures of our nations. Those decisions are and will be recorded in historical books for all to read and become knowledgeable about. But, the moments that I want to call to our attention are the moments that are significant to each individual. To each person that has been given life, they have also been given a purpose for that life and a time to pursue the purpose. Unfortunately, as beautiful as the gift of life is, there is also given the eternal enemy of life. The purpose of an enemy is to oppose, to kill, to steal, to destroy and to abort any meaningful purpose and bring its destruction into being. Life's ultimate enemy is of course, death. However, death is only the climax of the process of bringing to an end all forms of life.

Mankind, as well as the flowers and vegetation, birds, animals and reptiles all have a specific time span for existence. Death's process is quickened many times however by disease, wars, plagues, accidents and other misfortunes that occur for various reasons, sometimes beyond our comprehension. Nevertheless, with all of this being true, the grand scheme of things is not the focus of what I want to write about. Being of the Christian faith, I believe in the Supreme Being, the God of the whole universe, who with purpose in mind created everything. The scriptures of The Bible tell us that in the 'fullness' of time, God sent His Son to reconcile mankind back to Himself. If God had a purpose for sending His Son, then I believe that He had a purpose for each one of us that have received the breath of life.

I believe that we are not here by some accident, but by divine purpose. I believe somewhere in God's eternity past and in the 'fullness' of His time for humankind that our life, purpose and time span here on earth were created and allotted to each of us. For the purpose of this book however, I must leave my thoughts of the magnificence of the universal realm behind, and focus on not the whole of one's life, but on the moments that make up the memories of life's journey. We, being a part of the human race are alike in so many aspects, yet so different as individuals that none of us have identical fingerprints. This gives us reason to think each significant moment in one person's life will differ from significant moments in another's life.

We being individuals, are still part of the whole human race. Therefore, we are connected to other individuals by birth, adoption, marriage or some other connection. None of us are individual islands apart to ourselves. This connection wherein we have been joined together is the point I want to emphasize here. To someone, somewhere, we are or should be responsible, not responsible for, but to others. There has to have been a connection because we are children, grandchildren, aunts and uncles, nieces and nephews, moms and dads, and friends of some person or persons some-where. I believe that to someone our lives count and that we are truly cared for. We do matter to someone. This is the purpose of creating this book.

In life's journey, we get caught up in the situations of utter existence that times of gathering together to share life's experiences are sometimes few and far between. This leaves a void that may never get filled because time just doesn't permit many moments of intimate relationships. By not being able to verbalize our innermost thoughts and feelings, we may drift through life not really under-standing or being understood. Many facets of life are common to each one of us, but it is the MOMENTS that are precious to us as individuals, that sometimes go unnoticed and unrecognized until there is no more time to share.

This book is not intended to be a diary or personal journal. It is my desire that what I have written will become an incentive for people to record precious moments of their lives to share with those who they can now enjoy together or will leave for others who come after them. Thus, leaving a memoir of moments that we have treasured to become part of a better connection and understanding of who we are, how we have felt, and what sets us apart from other people (even close family members) will give others an opportunity to know us better, and perhaps appreciate the purpose of our life's journey here on earth.

Leaving room in the book to continue to record my own personal MOMENTS, I have given some examples of beautiful moments that to me are indeed too precious to forget. I hope you will be blessed as you reminisce through the archives of your memory and then find time now and in the future to record some of your life's MOMENTS TO REMEMBER that are, to you, 'Priceless and Too Precious to Forget'. Some of the moments you remember and encounter may not be happy and that is OK, it is the special moments that you may not ever get to share in person with anyone that is important. Sometimes, sad moments are worth remembering also, and are very special. It is each moment that has meant something special to you that you may wish to write down to share and hand down to those who follow you.

After each lined page in this book, there is a blank side for you to create your own personal way in which to remember the moment so special to you. You may want to insert your own special photo, etc., to personalize your MOMENTS TO REMEMBER. Which ever way you choose, let it be specific and special to you. It is how you have been affected in a specific moment that you want to share with those who will choose to read, understand, and remember what your life was about- even if it comes after your departure from this existence. May the peace and the blessings of the God of the whole universe be extended to you now and as time goes by. May you get the chance to record as many of the precious moments in your life as you possibly can and the memories of your existence be filled with precious moments to those who will follow you.

Moments to Remember

Moments to Remember

Dad

My dad was a horseman, and he always owned horses for as far back as I remember. His theory was if a child was old enough to walk, he was old enough to ride and up on the horse we went. It was a lot of fun though; sometimes he had all three of us kids, my brother and sister and me, on the horse at the same time. I guess that is why we all loved horses too. It was so sad when my dad had to give up caring for his horses. In the last few years of his life, he lived with me. He had developed cancer and I took care of him. On the day he died, there was one special moment I know that was just for me. I usually read something to him after lunch and before he took a nap in the afternoon. When I had finished reading that day, I checked to see if he needed anything. Assuring me that he was ok, he held my hand unusually firm and as he looked at me, there was a sparkle in his sky-blue eyes and the expression on his face was like a child trying to keep a secret. I remember as I left the room, such a bittersweet emotion came over me. I thought my heart would surely burst. As I looked back at him when I left his room, for some reason, I could not hold back the tears and I cried most of the afternoon. I didn't know then, but I realized later that night that what I had seen in his face and eyes and felt in his hand was his special "goodbye" to me. My dad passed away early that evening.

Moments to Remember

_____

_____

_____

_____

_____

_____

_____

_____

_____

_____

_____

_____

_____

_____

_____

_____

_____

_____

_____

_____

_____

_____

_____

Moments to Remember

_____
_____
_____
_____
_____
_____
_____
_____
_____
_____
_____
_____
_____
_____
_____
_____
_____
_____
_____
_____
_____
_____

Moments to Remember

Moments to Remember

Moments to Remember

Moments to Remember

Moments to Remember

Moments to Remember

Moments to Remember

Moments to Remember

Sandy

Moments to Remember

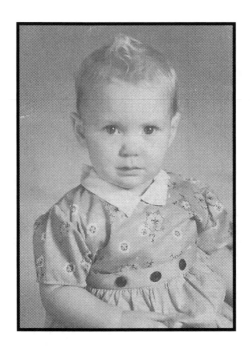

Sandy

I wonder how one might forget a moment that cannot be expressed in words. I remember during my pregnancy, all of the planning and imagining how it would be when the day would finally arrive. After all the preparation, waiting, and choosing and changing names, I finally had chosen the names I liked the most. But, I simply was not prepared to see my baby daughter for the first time. Awestruck is the best word I can use to describe that moment. I had been waiting with great antici- pation for the moment of her arrival. I had envisioned this tiny little red face with dark shaggy hair. After all didn't all new- born babies look alike, kind of anyway, right? Well, not so for this one. I remember the surprise and awe when I saw her. She was neither, tiny, red faced or dark haired. Her skin was so smooth and a beautiful creamy peach color, her hair was very short and blonde and she had such big beauti- ful eyes. During those first moments of bonding, elation, bliss and pure delight, I held her close and brushed my lips across her velvety soft hair, then a funny thought came to me, and that was, one thing I knew for sure, I would definitely have to change her name, ---AGAIN!!!

Moments to Remember

_____

_____

_____

_____

_____

_____

_____

_____

_____

_____

_____

_____

_____

_____

_____

_____

_____

_____

_____

_____

_____

_____

_____

Moments to Remember

Moments to Remember

_____

_____

_____

_____

_____

_____

_____

_____

_____

_____

_____

_____

_____

_____

_____

_____

_____

_____

_____

_____

_____

_____

_____

_____

_____

_____

_____

Moments to Remember

_____

_____

_____

_____

_____

Moments to Remember

_____

_____

_____

_____

_____

_____

_____

_____

_____

_____

_____

_____

_____

_____

_____

_____

_____

_____

_____

_____

_____

_____

_____

Moments to Remember

Moments to Remember

_____

_____

_____

_____

_____

_____

_____

_____

_____

_____

_____

_____

_____

_____

_____

_____

_____

_____

_____

_____

_____

_____

_____

_____

_____

_____

Moments to Remember

_____

_____

_____

_____

_____

_____

_____

_____

_____

_____

_____

_____

_____

_____

_____

_____

_____

_____

_____

_____

_____

_____

_____

_____

_____

_____

_____

_____

Moments to Remember

Moments to Remember

Moments to Remember

Heaven's Kiss

Moments to Remember

Heaven's Kiss

I am of the Christian faith and belief. In terms of denomination, probably classified as Pentecostal. I was driving home from my Bible study class one day; I was having a joyous time singing, praising and thanking the Lord for such a wonderful day. When I drove into my driveway, I remember saying "Oh I love you so much, Lord, you are so good to me" and then I just blew a kiss toward the sky. The sky was a beautiful blue with fluffy white clouds. Instantly, I saw a giant shape of a mouth form in the sky and seemed to draw substance from the clouds to make large lips that puckered. Suddenly, the lips opened and blew a big kiss back to me. It was so real, that I could almost hear the 'smack'. That was a most exciting moment for me and I hesitated to get out of the car. As, I kept my eyes skyward; I knew that I had made a spiritual contact and my heart simply over-flowed with joy and wonderment. I remember saying 'Wow, you are there, aren't you Lord?" I thought who would believe me if I told them of my experience, then I felt a loving peace and within my spirit I knew that it didn't matter because, the moment was meant especially for me.

Moments to Remember

_____

_____

_____

_____

_____

_____

_____

_____

_____

_____

_____

_____

_____

_____

_____

_____

_____

_____

_____

_____

_____

Moments to Remember

Moments to Remember

_____

_____

_____

_____

_____

_____

_____

_____

_____

_____

_____

_____

_____

_____

_____

_____

_____

_____

_____

_____

_____

Moments to Remember

_____

_____

_____

_____

_____

_____

_____

_____

_____

_____

_____

_____

_____

_____

_____

_____

_____

_____

_____

_____

_____

_____

Moments to Remember

Moments to Remember

Moments to Remember

_____

_____

_____

_____

_____

_____

_____

_____

_____

_____

_____

_____

_____

_____

_____

_____

_____

_____

_____

_____

_____

_____

_____

_____

Moments to Remember

_____

_____

_____

_____

_____

_____

_____

_____

_____

_____

_____

_____

_____

_____

_____

_____

_____

_____

_____

_____

_____

_____

_____

_____

_____

Moments to Remember

_____

_____

_____

_____

_____

_____

_____

_____

_____

_____

_____

_____

_____

_____

_____

_____

_____

_____

_____

_____

_____

_____

_____

_____

_____

_____

Moments to Remember

Moments to Remember

Penny

Moments to Remember

$\mathcal{P}enny$

Not all of the memories are happy, but are precious just the same. Such is the case with my dog, Penny. She was a beautiful lab mix and very dear to my heart. She loved the outdoors, swimming, making "snow angels" and walking in the moonlight was her favorite times. We liked walking in the snow and in the light of the full moon best. I liked to watch her frolic in the shadows when the moon shone through the trees, but making snow angels was her specialty. Sadly, in the last few months of her life she developed a terminal health problem. It was a battle that we couldn't win. It seems, though, that she chose a favorite time to go. It was at the end of October and it was a full moon.

As I stayed close by her that night, the moon was so big and shined so brightly into the room. She curled up in one of her favorite spots by the glass doors, I think, in order to lie in the moonlight. I knew that she was going to die and being determined that she would not be alone at the end of her life; I lay on the couch to be near her. In the bright moonlight, nearing the dawn, I heard her dreaming, or perhaps she was saying goodbye to me and then she decided to leave. I think she may have caught a glimpse of her friend and mentor, Rodney, who taught her to swim and play when she was a puppy, beckoning to her from " doggie heaven" and she just ran off to meet him in the moonlight and ran right out of this life without me. I can almost see the two of them as they raced off into the heavens, leaving me with only the precious memories of our time together.

Moments to Remember

_____
_____
_____
_____
_____
_____
_____
_____
_____
_____
_____
_____
_____
_____
_____
_____
_____
_____
_____
_____
_____
_____
_____
_____

Moments to Remember

_____

_____

_____

_____

_____

_____

_____

_____

_____

_____

_____

_____

_____

_____

_____

_____

_____

_____

_____

_____

_____

_____

_____

_____

_____

Moments to Remember

Moments to Remember

Moments to Remember

Moments to Remember

_____
_____
_____
_____
_____

_____
_____
_____
_____
_____
_____
_____
_____
_____
_____
_____
_____
_____
_____
_____
_____
_____
_____
_____
_____

Moments to Remember

_____
_____
_____
_____
_____

_____
_____
_____
_____
_____
_____
_____
_____
_____
_____
_____
_____
_____
_____
_____
_____
_____
_____
_____

Moments to Remember

_____

_____

_____

_____

_____

_____

_____

_____

_____

_____

_____

_____

_____

_____

_____

_____

_____

_____

_____

_____

_____

_____

_____

_____

_____

_____

_____

Moments to Remember

_____

_____

_____

_____

_____

_____

_____

_____

_____

_____

_____

_____

_____

_____

_____

_____

_____

_____

_____

_____

_____

_____

_____

_____

_____

Moments to Remember

_____

_____

_____

_____

_____

_____

_____

_____

_____

_____

_____

_____

_____

_____

_____

_____

_____

_____

_____

_____

_____

_____

_____

_____

_____

_____

_____

_____

_____

_____

Grandad, It's a Trout!

Moments to Remember

Grandad, It's a Trout!

One day, when my grandson Brandon was around 4-5 years old, I took him fishing. He caught a small brook trout and we took it home. He couldn't wait to show my dad his fish. "Granddaddy it's a trout!" he exclaimed, as he held it up for my dad to see. My dad was impressed with the fish and said to Brandon, "Well, we'll just clean him up and have him for supper." I was in the kitchen when I heard Brandon coming through the dining room. As I looked around, there he stood with the fish in his hands and soap suds dripping onto the floor. He had taken the fish into the bathroom and washed it. His voice was filled with joy and excitement as he asked me, "Is he clean enough, Gram?" The expression on his face was priceless. The look on my dad's face was priceless too as he could not hold back the laughter. Winking at me, he complimented Brandon on such a fine job of cleaning "him". Then, they went off to talk about how he caught it and although it took a bit of extra cleaning, they did have trout for supper. From the conversation at the supper table, it was one delicious trout.

Moments to Remember

Moments to Remember

Moments to Remember

Moments to Remember

Moments to Remember

_____

_____

_____

_____

_____

_____

_____

_____

_____

_____

_____

_____

_____

_____

_____

_____

_____

_____

_____

_____

_____

_____

_____

Moments to Remember

Moments to Remember

Moments to Remember

Moments to Remember

Moments to Remember

Capture The Moment

Moments to Remember

Capture the Moment

How precious are the moments of spontaneity, when someone we love surprises us with a special gift. This was especially true with Brandon. He was very spontaneous with his affection when he was small and chose to show much honest and innocent affection to those he loved by placing a kiss on their cheek or a big hug around the neck. Sometimes, we are fortunate enough to have a camera handy to capture a specific moment. This was the case when my little grandson, Brandon, was about 2 ½. My daughter just happened to be handy with the camera when Brandon decided to show his little cousin Lisa how much he loved her, and he surprised her with a big kiss. There are many moments that I shall remember of his spontaneous gifts of affection, but I treasure this moment because his mom captured it to keep forever.

Moments to Remember

Moments to Remember

_____
_____
_____
_____
_____
_____
_____
_____
_____
_____
_____
_____
_____
_____
_____
_____
_____
_____
_____
_____
_____
_____
_____
_____
_____
_____

Moments to Remember

_____

_____

_____

_____

_____

_____

_____

_____

_____

_____

_____

_____

_____

_____

_____

_____

_____

_____

_____

_____

_____

_____

_____

_____

_____

_____

_____

Moments to Remember

_____

_____

_____

_____

_____

_____

_____

_____

_____

_____

_____

_____

_____

_____

_____

_____

_____

_____

_____

_____

_____

_____

_____

_____

Moments to Remember

_____

Moments to Remember

_____

_____

_____

_____

_____

_____

_____

_____

_____

_____

_____

_____

_____

_____

_____

_____

_____

_____

_____

_____

_____

_____

_____

_____

Moments to Remember

_____
_____
_____
_____
_____

_____
_____
_____
_____
_____
_____
_____
_____
_____
_____
_____
_____
_____
_____
_____
_____
_____
_____
_____
_____
_____
_____
_____

Moments to Remember

_____

_____

_____

_____

_____

_____

_____

_____

_____

_____

_____

_____

_____

_____

_____

_____

_____

_____

_____

_____

_____

_____

_____

_____

_____

_____

_____

Moments to Remember

Moments to Remember

Goodbye Friend

Moments to Remember

Goodbye Friend

From time to time, I work in the Health Care field, but sometimes I just volunteer as a companion and friend. Mostly, being a friend to an elderly person. Lots of times a person finds themselves near the end of life and alone. Doris was such a person. I used to visit with her quite often and we became good friends. As the end drew nearer for her, she became more afraid of being alone. Although, she had home care aides she was personally very lonely and afraid. I remember, one evening I helped her into bed, she wanted to keep talking. So, I lingered by her bedside for a long while, as she chatted away. But, the next morning her aide called to tell me that she had been admitted to the hospital. I went to the hospital to see her early that day, she was so small and frail lying there. But, when she saw me a big smile crossed her lips and she whispered, "Hi, you are my friend, and I knew you'd come". We talked for a few minutes, then she grew very peaceful and dozed off to sleep. So, as not to disturb her I quietly left. A very short while after I had gone, I felt a strange, yet beautiful feeling in my heart and I knew she had departed. It was a time of joy for me though, just to know that my visit to see her had somehow helped her to make a peaceful exit from this life.

Moments to Remember

Moments to Remember

_____

_____

_____

_____

_____

_____

_____

_____

_____

_____

_____

_____

_____

_____

_____

_____

_____

_____

_____

_____

_____

_____

_____

_____

_____

Moments to Remember

Moments to Remember

Moments to Remember

Moments to Remember

Moments to Remember

Moments to Remember

Moments to Remember

Moments to Remember

Farewell

drawing by Brandon Thompson

Farewell

Shortly after I lost my dog Penny, who was certainly my friend and companion, I received this poem. It brought a moment of relief, and made the pain of her leaving more bearable. I would like to pass it on to you.

Farewell

Farewell master, yet not farewell

For where I have gone, you too shall dwell

Gone from before your face

A moments time, a little space

But when you come to where I have stepped

You will wonder why you wept.

-Anonymous

Moments to Remember

Moments to Remember

Moments to Remember

Moments to Remember

Moments to Remember

Moments to Remember

Moments to Remember

Moments to Remember

Moments to Remember

Moments to Remember

Printed in the United States
By Bookmasters